Bible Belt Revolution

a collection of poetry
by Julianne King

King, Julianne
1st Edition
ISBN: 978-1-7378279-2-4
"a moment of hate" first appeared in the South Florida Poetry
Journal in cine form in the August 2020 edition.

For every survivor.

Part I - Burn it all down.

Part II - Where was my body again?

Part I - Burn it all down.

to the establishment.

The she, the he, the them, the they,
the I, the we
don't
give
a fuck
what you think
you didn't want our voices raised
when jobs dried up
when we tried to save some turtles
or asked that the world not
turn our grandchildren to dust
You didn't want our input on our lives
as adults
and what it would look like when you
all
took your places in graves we dug for
the word
"experience" to display for the next
hoping it lands us somewhere clear of
hungry

You didn't hear our little brothers and
sisters
turn whispers to battle cries when
bullets
kept piercing the lives you swore to us
you were protecting
keeping us safe from all the dangers
out
there

but you didn't want to hear our ideas
about the shift in the world
we live in

as long as your millions stayed safe
with accountants in banks somewhere far
offshore
You kept your place in the Hamptons or
Dubai or Cali and let people go hungry
believing it to be the fault of not
trying hard enough
but all we have done is try
and adapt and change the world to keep
pace
but that was also an affront to your
notion of us being kept in our place
which is to say out of your place
under your feet
under your thumb
and enough will never be enough
greed like air to feed you
but every life has a limit and when you
have aged yourself out of existence
out of relevance, we will finally get
our chance to build something better.

But I hope we don't

for the world will have shifted again

I hope we learn, let go, turn it over
with joy to a generation possessing the
thing that you stole-

hope

whet.

I am all done
with tight-lipped culture
if my lips are not whetted,
free to convey all my thoughts and
desires
you are not putting in the time
to listen
too afraid to hear the truth:
the smallness of me
will not increase
the girth of you
or your words
or your deeds.
I am not here to magnify you.
Loose lips do not sink ships
big, thick, penetrating
icebergs do.
So don't stand in judgment of these
well-worked lips,
this strong-muscled
jaw
stand instead beside a mirror and
realize
you do not encompass the world entire.
There is room.
Do your job
and make it.

MDE.

I am sure
you have all heard
of Big Dick Energy
That *I know what I have*
You know who I am energy
That *I will make your girl scream* aura
spooned on like honey or sweat or
throbbing
heartbeats,
turn every head
easily in command
Trust me I've got this swagger.
But I'm about to
introduce you
to something different
Medium Dick Energy.
I am absolutely sure
you've seen it a time or two
you will recognize for instance
the puffed chest, squared shoulder
strut
a little too obvious
to anyone who looks.
The big show, loud voice frantic
motions to mimic the movements
that intimidated them.
This is MDE at its finest,
the loudest and brightest, *keep your*
woman quiet and alone energy
throw a punch to prove a point—maybe--
Who knows?
MDEs are masters of disguise and
distractions
unable to attract any attention

based on proof.
They can't hang
with the big boys so they play in the
shallows
staying in the shadows until
the right prey emerges.
I implore all my male-loving cohorts
to take this message to heart:
Medium Dick Energy is dangerous--
push the button because I can mess,
start a war with my orange thumbs,
bless the abusers and condemn the
lovers,
drop a child like an old iPhone
caress you but only use you up until
there is nothing left
dangerous.
But hear this:
the pinprick of kryptonite
to their under-inflated *personality*
size is the truth
and two little words
Prove it.

the confirmation of 2020.

Early morning conversation with my cat:

Are you sure you want to go out there?
it's cold.
winter is almost here.
i can't protect you.
okay.
fine then.
but don't say i didn't warn you.

radical.

It is not pro life
to raise birth rates
but not children
It is not pro life
to cheer an execution
like delivering
raw turkey
to homes with
no ovens and
celebrating the
generous Thanksgiving

It is not pro life
to arm the masses
when mob rule means
more and more and
more deaths

It is not pro life
to hike prices
but not wages
It is not pro life
to profit us out of existence

You are pro birth
because there is nothing
lower than murder
except watching another
child starve with the others

You are pro birth
to hell with the already living
and the chains of uterine slavery

capitalists always focus
on production and not outcome

Please
Be pro *life*
make deliveries safer
adopt a child
from a mother who cannot
support her
hold them up when life
turns sour for a month
or a decade
or at least keep the women
you're enslaving
in high rises so the
price of their fertility is
equal to the loss of their autonomy

Reward their prized ovaries
for bringing blessings when
thirty percent of the time they will
give
their
lives.
But wait
haven't we seen this with red dresses
and hand maids.

Be Pro Life
be a church that cares for a child
let willing, loving parents adopt
or unload the gun
his jeans carry so that
maybe she

doesn't have to choose
Please

for the love of your god
Be
Pro
Life

silence.

Some women learn their silence at the
dinner table before their milk teeth
have been offered for quarters.

Some in church pews when verses are
used to explain why God doesn't want
them leading anything other than the
baby race.

Others find it in the backseats of old
cars when expectations and groping
hands find justification and she gives
in because *he's put in the time*.

I learned mine the hard way,
came to it the long way 'round when
voice after voice drowned out my
opinion, mocked my knowledge and
challenged my capacity for kindness
when I dared to ask for more than
thirty percent of the oxygen in the
room.

I learned to stay silent when every
need I clearly expressed in every
language my body could conjure was
ignored
every hope trampled
every day a new heartbreak as line
after line was dismissed, erased
altogether under the guise of my needs
being wants, my lines being dotted--
dashed on a highway,

suggestions to be crossed when
convenient for the drivers of cars that
wrecked my
life again
and again
and again
like I hadn't even spoken at all,
as though I'd never said clearly *that
hurt me*
like my theatre-trained voice wasn't
loud enough to carry
two injuries rolled into one--
the hurt
and the betrayal that comes when
clearly defined, lovingly guided lines
are erased like a child's chalked sun
driven out by the rain.
I stopped speaking then,
stopped stitching broken hearts onto my
sleeve for them to use against me
I learned that nothing good came from
honesty
or clarity
or hope.
I found my needs could be locked inside
and kill me only once.

I gave into my place
I breathed away my anger and cut
diatribes into scars on my body instead
of engaging and revealing my tender,
beating, broken wound
I took twenty-eight years
the long way 'round
But even I learned silence.

i'm fine.

i'm sorry
i had a breakdown
at your house
again
i've been having
a lot of those
lately
but i'm fine.
it's fine.
i'm fine.

little girl.

She's around here
somewhere-
the little girl
innocent
hopeful.
She's here calling
for me.
I've heard her
every night
since she went
missing,
fading into cruel reality,
aging into this
cynical
woman.

bible belt.

In the middle of my liberal-leaning,
feminist-only, mostly queer, self-aware
circle it's easy to forget where I come
from: The Bible Belt.

Corn-fed, Barefoot Baptist, keep your
personal life to yourself glory unless
your secret
is a secret child, then they want you
to know there are choices so they can
tell you God hates baby killers and
shame you into
labor while they sit at dinner and
scold the cretins who take handouts
like food stamps and Medicaid.
So many choices.

They want the best for their children
They want to live to be one hundred but
cigarettes and automatics are God-given
rights redoubled by the Constitution
which is infallible in its amendments.

They keep their daughters safe at
night, teach them to defend themselves
and hope the world is kind.

They taught us that kindness comes
easiest to the pretty and compliant. It

wasn't to trap us but to keep us safe
and easy, making babies to raise in the
Heartland with our husbands because in
their minds, everyone gets to outlive
their youthful indiscretions.

They are funny and witty. Some even
have their college degrees and
retirement funds to hang like merit
badges from chests
hunched over the back-breaking work
that pays the bills.

They are heroes and humble unless
politics are discussed and even then
it's because they truly believe they
know best. For everyone.

Racism doesn't exist to them because
they would never make a dark-skinned
man drink from a different fountain but
they will talk about how wild *those*
people act. Like thugs. Like animals.
We would never behave like that. They
teach their children blind faith in
authority is the only logical option

and forget entirely the summer they
told them to drive miles if needed to

the nearest lit business if lights
flashed in the rearview or else risk
being assaulted like those other girls.

They fervently hold onto phrases like
*God will not give you more than you can
handle* but seem to have skipped the
book of Job.

These people cook Christmas supper and
give to charity from checks that barely
keep the lights on and pray for babies
but won't teach their children how to
survive a chemical imbalance.

They are doing their best, like all of
us, to do what they believe is upright
and moral. I forget sometimes that
their world is small enough to make
them think they are succeeding.

They don't have to make room in their
ideology for someone who loves like me
because their god printed a get out of
jail free card in the 1450s.

They don't have to listen to the pain
of the next generation because suicides
aren't soldiers even though the

battlefield is in every classroom.

Good people with good intentions are
watching the world burn because the
smoke doesn't reach to the Bootheel.
Because good people with good
intentions will not rise against the
manifestation of their destiny;
because good people with good
intentions cannot be bothered to part
with the teaching of their preachers
and read the good book for themselves

because they just might think for
themselves and readers and thinkers are
dangerous creatures in the Bible Belt
where *Over my dead body* applies to
their armory, but the dead bodies
piling up are their children
and still they talk of tyranny and how
that can never happen again forgetting
Columbine and Sandy Hook, Virginia Tech
and Parkland, and Meramec Valley Middle
School where four threats in three
months is normal.

Over and over the dead bodies of dead
children who die from abuse and

neglect, from their **own** hands when
their **own** family tells them they are an
abomination.
Trigger fingers over children.

Faith over humanity, over the shells of
the victims laid at their feet by
priests' hands when the whole
institution should be dismantled brick
by brick.

We should be paving roads with the
bones of the Vatican but faith and guns
are guarded by the kind, by the up
Right, by the good.

How high will they rise before they
realize they are standing on the bones
of good people with good intentions who
just wanted to live?

fog.

Congratulations on having the right mix
of chemicals in your brain
your father must be so
proud
what an accomplishment
Did you opt for the plaque or the
pocket watch?
Watch my eyes glitter with jealousy,
with lust for how hard you must
have worked
Your mama sure did raise you right
and the bootstraps you
pulled yourself up with must be the
shit
Too bad they aren't for lease to the
weak-
minded like me
That's what you see here right?

Wait, I'm sorry. Let me
start again.

How to explain depression fog
to Normies.
Step One:
Don't. No really.
Let yourself off the hook because
how can you ever explain that some days
you can go to work with
the flu and two broken feet, but some
days
standing up from the couch makes your
heartbeat hurt your chest and sleep

is the only thing that makes sense but
you know that's making everything
worse
so you just lie there paralyzed in the
dark.
It's not their fault.
They can't
understand. Their brains just happen
to manufacture
the things they need to get up day
after day without exhaustion
that reaches back into their youth,
stealing their ability to stand.
Don't
envy them. Just live from bed.
That's all you have to
do today my love, just live

And then when you raze yourself
from bed and find the world
still wants to know why you don't work
that way
you can tell them all to fuck
off or tell them

Congratulations!
Where did you get your certificate
of normal? Polo?
Your mama sure did raise you
right

new day.

once i stopped
hating myself
i started holding
others
Accountable too.

Part II - Where was my body again?

dissociate.

I wish
more than anything
that I could feel
you
twist the knife.

I cannot even
feel the body
your knife
slid into.

i want to be her.

Women who are large in their bodies,
whose self reaches all the way to their
fingertips
who occupy every inch of their
spreading thighs
and untremulous voices
these are the women who make me know I
am not small,
I am not meek,
I am not subservient.
My place among them is a place
predestined by the stars
by the earth and the blood that bore us
forward,
by the moon who is our mother, and the
water that calls us home.
My place existed before I was myself
made mother,
before my belly and breasts filled with
life,
before my first blood or my first bra.

I am therefore I am.

Whole. Complete.
Not half a man set to make us into a
being.
This is the reason belly lines and
cellulite
ring church bells in my soul right
alongside pear-shaped hips and perfect
breasts beneath my hands.

Because the package does not define the
woman contained within
no matter what they tell us or try to
sell us to make us feel enough.
The package cannot contain us, cannot
keep us small forever,
forever hidden inside, shrinking inward
to make room for others,
to be good girls with our legs closed
and our makeup on point.
Those walls cannot hold someone like
her who reaches to the edge of her skin
and beyond,
changing the emotional temperature of
every room she enters,
cannot lessen the lesson her spirit
imparts
by Being,
by Existing.

This is the woman I want to be:
The one who extends all the way to the
tips of my fingers
to my reflection
to my stretch marks and violin hips

I want to fill the space that is me,
live in it and know I have given the
world a gift by choosing to live-
by choosing to do the boring things
like take my pills and wash my hair
and love myself
-by living

start something.

sharp tongue
bootheel mind
rooftop fists

I'm a goddamn
Weapon.
pointed.

Yeah.

I wanna start
something.

a moment of hate.

Dudes. Fucking men.
all superiority and no priorities
no common sense
telling you there are
a hundred women
waiting to fuck
your
girl
better and longer
to teach her the part of her you use
is the part they will worship,
build a temple
just to sample
her beauty
-a gasp, a shock, dis-
belief that you won't lose her to a
dude, but to me
or to her high school sweetheart [sic]
best friend
who taught her love doesn't have to be
hard,
to the best friend [sic] first love who
showed
her love is not a code
she must crack
but a gift I will plant
in the garden at her feet
where I meet
to worship her daily.

I'm beginning to think the wage gap
is just another way that you
keep us parted.
look what would be if our wants
and not our needs

brought us together.
would you weather the storm? or
are deep pockets and dick pics
the best you can bring her
and tell her it's dinner
and shove yourself further
into a space she doesn't have for you.
I guess this is my coming out
and a petulance about
a gender
but you're right
not all men fit under this title
I just wish none of them did.
I wish our value
was more than the parts we supply.
that's the reason all you dudes
all you guys
have to step it up
because the shit you're slinging
is no longer enough.

We are more than vaginas and vulvas and
clits you can't find
and now is your time to evolve.
advance.
give yourself a fighting chance
because it's not just the dude at the
gym
coming for your girl,
I am.

why women cut their hair after a breakup.

Because we fucking want to
that's why
because we kept our strands long
when you begged us not to cut them
every summer when we grew tired
and annoyed by the upkeep
But we were tired
and annoyed by your upkeep and we kept
you

by comparison
the hair wasn't much more to ask

because we kept a style you asked for
in your not-so-subtle jabs at the
young women
with the
short hair
*Don't they know how pretty they could
be?*

We do it so that our time away from
you,
our distance from the trauma
can be measured in length that belongs
to us alone
Hair that your fingers
did not run through
that you did not play with
as we fell asleep on your chest
did not carry
our scent

to your nose
Just as we look forward to that
mythical moment
seven years from your leaving
when every cell in our bodies
has turned over,
been renewed
and we will stand knowing you
have never touched us at all
and our bodies
will once again
belong to us

your hands did not touch
This Skin
your fingers did not grope
These Breasts
you did not run your fingers

through This Hair

This Hair belongs to me.
This Hair belongs to me.

wonderland.

My body is not
a wonderland
but a pile of ashes
I keep stacking in the shape
of a person.